Sleeping WITH THE Enemy

Sleeping WITH THE *Enemy*

THE DEVIL'S LIES
TO TODAY'S FAMILIES

Melvin S. Baker, LMSW

WESTBOW
PRESS®
A DIVISION OF THOMAS NELSON
& ZONDERVAN

WestBow Press books may be ordered through booksellers or by contacting:

WestBow Press
A Division of Thomas Nelson & Zondervan
1663 Liberty Drive
Bloomington, IN 47403
www.westbowpress.com
1 (866) 928-1240

KJV: Scripture taken from the King James Version of the Bible.

ISBN: 978-1-9736-6686-8 (sc)
ISBN: 978-1-9736-6685-1 (e)

Library of Congress Control Number: 2019908333

Print information available on the last page.

WestBow Press rev. date: 6/25/2019

For the son dishonoureth the father, the daughter riseth up against her mother, the daughter-in-law against her mother in law; **a man's enemies are the men of his own house.**

—*Micah 7:6 (KJV)*

INTRODUCTION

In the book of Ephesians, the apostle Paul writes a wonderful letter to the church at Ephesus concerning the things of God. Among the many topics addressed in this particular letter are the redemptive work of Jesus, salvation given by grace, the operation and cooperation of ministerial gifts and offices, and marital submission. Paul begins the final chapter with words of instruction for the family unit:

> Children obey your parents in the Lord: for this is right. Honour thy father and mother; which is the first commandment with promise; that it may be well with thee, and thou mayest live long on the earth. (Ephesians 6:1–3 KJV)

It is critical that we understand and embrace the fact that in this passage, Paul was speaking to children about their relationship with their parents in the context of their attitudes and actions.

Oftentimes, there is a misconception that Paul was speaking

to youth as opposed to children in a passage of scripture. The difference between the two is that *youth* speaks of a particular time in an individual's life while *children* speaks of a position that an individual assumes at conception that lasts throughout one's life. Consider the following verse:

> Remember NOW thy Creator IN THE DAYS OF THY YOUTH, while the evil days come not, nor the years draw nigh, when thou shalt say, I have no pleasure in them. (Ecclesiastes 12:1 KJV)

The expression "...IN THE DAYS OF THY YOUTH.." refers to a person's childhood and adolescence. Notice the urgency in Solomon's words as he encourages readers to give diligence to establishing a personal relationship with God their Creator. Meanwhile, in Ephesians 6:1, while Paul's words of instruction include individuals in their youth, they speak to all.

Some adult readers may be wondering about the purpose of all this explanation. One reason I have included it is that we sometimes, as adults, lose sight of our God-given responsibilities as children to honor and respect our parents. We develop a level of self-sufficiency that in many cases breeds pride and irreverence toward our parents. In the process, we forget that our obedience, honor, and reverence are to be maintained out of our love for God and reverential consideration of the God-given position our parents hold in our lives.

It is my belief that comprehension of this topic is critical to the end-times Church. For as much as marriage is the

cornerstone of today's family, strong godly households serve as the foundation for vibrant, life-changing ministries. Growing up, some of the tragedies I witnessed were the dividing of church assemblies, disputes among church leadership, and despising of church brethren. Though in many cases these issues yet remain, I have noticed somewhat of a transition of division and detriment from the church house to the houses that make up the church.

Our churches are now made up of families that reflect the following passage:

> For the son dishonoureth the father, the daughter riseth up against her mother, the daughter in law against her mother in law; a man's enemies are the men of his own house. (Micah 7:6 KJV)

Our churches have transitioned into fellowships with fragmented homes where parents and children inflict so much harm on each other. The Old Testament prophet Micah likens the hostility and discord that so many of our families are encountering to warfare. The individuals we are living with have started to look like our enemies.

When I think about the words of this passage of scripture, it seems ironic that the individuals who have been designed to be our source of love and support are perceived as our source of conflict, adversity, pain, and ultimately our greatest threat of death. It is the aforementioned dynamics that have inspired me, by the grace of God and the leading of the Holy Ghost, to

write this book. Oftentimes, as members of a family, we are hostile toward one another, and we are either ignorant of or fail to recognize the devil's agenda to destroy our relationships with our families.

CHAPTER 1

God's Intentions for Marriage

Therefore shall a man leave his father and his
mother; and shall cleave unto his wife: and they shall
be one flesh. And they were both naked, the man
and his wife, and WERE NOT ASHAMED.
                                    —*Genesis 2:24–25 (KJV)*

And thou shalt teach them diligently unto thy
children, and shalt talk of them when thou sittest in
thine house, and when thou walkest by the way, and
when thou liest down, and when thou risest up.
                                    —*Deuteronomy 6:7 (KJV)*

G enesis 2:24–25 speaks of many things concerning
the institution called marriage. It speaks of the level
of intimacy that God intended for those who have entered
into marriage: "They shall be one flesh. And they were both

naked … and were not ashamed." In other words, Adam and Eve were close in association, knowledgeable of each other (familiar), and had established an undeniable level of comfort with each other's company. Given the fact that God handcrafted this union unlike any other marital union, it is safe to assume that these are some of the essential qualities necessary for a successful marriage.

The statement "Therefore shall a man leave his father and his mother" speaks of a transition of priority and responsibility. It speaks to the fact that when an individual gets married, he or she must realize the importance of his or her spouse and commitment to the marital union as the number-one responsibility with respect to human relationships. This can be easier said than done, because it demands a shift of priority for many of us. Also, this level of commitment requires one to make a conscious decision to enter into a lifestyle of humility and self-discipline.

The statement "and were not ashamed" speaks of a liberty that Adam and Eve discovered with each other in the institution of marriage. It reveals a level of grace that had not been present until God established the marital union. It also points to a level of self-discovery for Adam as he beheld his bride (Eve) for the first time.

In addition to Genesis 2:24–25, the Bible speaks of God's intention with regard to spousal attitude and interaction in Ephesians 5:22–33:

> Wives, submit yourselves unto your own husbands, as unto the Lord. For the husband is

the head of the wife, even as Christ is the head of the church: and he is the saviour of the body. Therefore, as the church is subject unto Christ, so let the wives be to their own husbands in everything. Husbands, love your wives, even as Christ also loved the church, and gave himself for it; That he might sanctify and cleanse it with the washing of water by the word, That he might present it to himself a glorious church, not having spot, or wrinkle, or any such thing; but that it should be holy and without blemish. So ought men to love their wives as their own bodies. He that loveth his wife loveth himself. For no man ever yet hated his own flesh; but nourisheth and cherisheth it, even as the Lord the church: For we are members of his body, of his flesh, and of his bones. For this cause shall a man leave his father and mother, and shall be joined unto his wife, and they two shall be one flesh. This is a great mystery: but I speak concerning Christ and the church. Nevertheless let every one of you in particular so love his wife even as himself; and the wife see that she reverence her husband. (KJV)

This scripture reveals God's plan and desire for husband and wife, as Paul likens the marital covenant to the covenant

relationship that Christ has established with the church, which is His bride.

In Ephesians 4:22, Paul instructs wives to consider their husbands God-given authority figures in their lives: "Wives, submit yourselves unto your own husbands, as unto the Lord." The word *submit* means to give over or yield to the power or authority of another; to present for the approval, consideration, or decision of another or others; to defer to another's judgment, opinion, or decision; and to allow oneself to be subjected to some kind of treatment. In other words, the apostle Paul is instructing wives to make the conscientious decision to allow themselves to become open to the direction, opinions, judgments, considerations, and treatment of their husbands.

The statement "as unto the Lord" speaks to the God-intended attitude of wives as they submit unto their husbands. It refers to our reverence and love for the omnipresent Lord. *Omnipresent* refers to God being ever-present in all places and spaces of time. *Lord* refers to God being in the highest position, particularly in one's life. To say that God is your Lord is to suggest that He is the most important being in your life, and there is nothing you would not do please Him. Paul writes "as unto the Lord" admonishing wives to submit to their husbands as if they are submitting themselves to the Lord.

In Ephesians 4:23, Paul writes that it is vital for wives to understand the proper perception and approach in dealing with their husbands: "For the husband is the head of the wife, even as Christ is the head of the church: and he is the saviour of the body." This verse provides women with a further explanation

and understanding of the husband-wife connection. In this verse alone, Paul explains God's intention for the husband to provide service, leadership, and protection for his wife. In Ephesians 4:24, Paul uses the dynamics of the relationship the church has with Christ as an example the wife is to model with regard to her attitude and interaction with her husband.

In Ephesians 4:25, Paul clearly defines the husband's responsibility to his wife: "Love your wives." Some might compare and contrast Paul's exhortation to the husband and wife and conclude that he puts more pressure on the wife. But that's not true. There is no greater responsibility given unto humanity than to love. Furthermore, when one considers the standard of love that Paul presents, it is abundantly clear that the greater task is laid before the husband. The standard of love is "even as Christ loved the church, and gave himself for it."

Oftentimes, the love of Christ is glamorized, but when Paul compares the love of a husband to the love that Christ demonstrated for His bride, the church, it is sobering and humbling. Consider this: Jesus is a man who faced all temptations yet successfully maintained the righteous standard of God, His Heavenly Father. Jesus makes a series of painful decisions—allowing Himself to be taken by His accusers; allowing His persecutors to nail His hands and feet; allowing Himself to be pierced in His side; allowing His persecutors to press a crown of thorns into His head—so He can demonstrate His love for His unrighteous and at times ungrateful bride in the belief that love would transform His bride.

The following verses in particular pull my memory to Paul's presentation on love in his first letter to the Corinthian church:

> Though I speak with the tongues of men and angels, and have not charity (love), I am become as sounding brass, or a tinkling cymbal. And though I have the gift of prophecy, and understand all mysteries, and all knowledge; and though I have all faith, so that I could remove mountains, and have not charity, I am nothing. And though I bestow all my goods to feed the poor, and though I give my body to be burned, and have not charity, it profiteth me nothing. Charity suffereth long, and is kind; charity envieth not; charity vaunteth not itself, is not puffed up. Doth not behave itself unseemly, seeketh not her own, is not easily provoked, thinketh no evil; Rejoiceth not in iniquity, but rejoiceth in the truth; Beareth all things, believeth all things, hopeth all things, endureth all things, Charity never faileth. (1 Corinthians 13:1–8)

> That he might sanctify and cleanse it with the washing of water by the word, that he might present it to himself a glorious church, not having spot, or wrinkle, or any such thing; but

that it should be holy and without blemish. (Ephesians 5:26–27)

In these scriptures, Paul presents the husband as the atmosphere-setter of the relationship. We see that it is Christ's responsibility as the bridegroom to usher His bride to her rightful position and condition as a clean, glorious, and holy bride: "That he might present it to himself a glorious church, not having spot, or wrinkle, or any such thing; but it should be holy and without blemish."

In the same way, Paul exhorts husbands to understand the vitality of their position in relation to the nature of the marital relationship. In Ephesians 5:26–27, we see the Bridegroom's (Christ's) love invoking the very best in His bride (the church). Oh, what a task—but do know, men of God, that for every instruction, God has already provided the necessary grace for us to obey Him and fulfill this call.

In Ephesians 5:28–29, Paul writes:

> So ought men to love their wives as their own bodies. He that loveth his wife loveth himself. For no man ever yet hated his own flesh; but nourisheth and cherisheth it, even as the Lord the church.

There is to be no difference between the love a husband has for himself and for his wife. In fact, the way the husband loves and cares for himself is to be the same measure of love that

he extends to his wife. After all, the Bible does declare that marriage unites two individuals.

> For this cause shall a man leave his father and mother, and shall be joined unto his wife, and they two shall be ONE FLESH. (Ephesians 5:31 KJV)

CHAPTER 2

God's Intention for Parents and Children

Children, obey your parents in the Lord: for this is
right. Honour thy father and mother; which is the first
commandment with promise; that it may be well with
thee, and thou mayest live long on the earth. And ye
fathers, provoke not your children to wrath: but bring
them up in the nurture and admonition of the Lord.
                                      —*Ephesians 6:1-4 (KJV)*

In my introductory statements, I spoke about the difference
between children and youth. I also mentioned the tendency
of adults to lose sight of the fact that they are someone's child,
even when their season of youth has expired. In this chapter,
I want to discuss the importance of maintaining parental
reverence throughout your life. In Ephesians 6:1, Paul writes,
"Children, obey your parents in the Lord: for this is right"

(KJV), providing us with instruction, strategy, and explanation concerning God's intention for children's attitudes toward and interaction with their parents. The instruction is rather clear: obey your parents.

The words "in the Lord" speak of the God-given strategy. They establish our relationship with the Lord Jesus Christ as the inspiration and sustaining factor of our obedience and honor toward our parents. In other words, as a child, I obey and honor my parents not because of the perfection of their actions but because they occupy a God-given position in my life. Further, the words "for this is right" summarize God's response to any possible human rebuttal to such a commandment. They also usher us toward a path that we as believers can pursue in our endeavor to please our God.

In Ephesians 6:2–3, Paul writes, "Honour thy father and mother; which is the first commandment with promise; that it may be well with thee, and thou mayest live long on the earth" (KJV). He is reminding us of the Old Testament commandment and the lifelong promise tied to it. The first verse here reminds us that our focus as children must be upon the fact that our parents occupy a God-given position. One of the lies of the enemy is that honoring the position of a father and mother is no longer important.

In addition to Paul's encouragement of the believers at Ephesus to remain mindful of the position of their parents, not perfection of character, he reminds them that this particular commandment sets the tone for their lives. The passage "which is the first commandment with promise; that it may be well

with thee, and thou mayest live long on the earth" reveals to us that our relationship with our parents serves the cornerstone of a person's life.

In Ephesians 6:4, Paul writes: "And ye fathers, provoke not your children to wrath: but bring them up in the nurture and admonition of the Lord" (KJV). Here, he extends words of caution and instruction to parents concerning their impact on their children. The amplified version of Ephesians 6:4 states, "Fathers, do not irritate and provoke your children to [do not exasperate them to resentment], but rear them [tenderly] in the training and discipline and the counsel and admonition of the Lord." The warning Paul extends to parents is to be careful not to become a source of irritation and anger for their children. In fact, Paul admonishes parents to raise their children with godly tenderness.

The words "in the nurture and admonition of the Lord" place a level of responsibility upon parents to be a source and model of godly love and behavior. The nurture of the Lord speaks of the dependency that exists within the parent-child relationship. For just as a little child nurses from his mother's breast, there is a dependency that exists throughout the lives of parents and their children. The nurture of the Lord speaks of the grace that God extends to us as His children. It also speaks of the Father's omniscience. He knows that we are not perfect and that in order for us to mature, He will have to be patient with us. In the same way, it is important for parents to always be conscious of the fact that their children are not perfect, and it is essential that their patience endure above and beyond their children's imperfections.

CHAPTER 3

The Devil's Agenda

Ye are of your father the devil, and the lusts of
your father ye will do. He was a murderer from the
beginning, and abode not in the truth, because there is
no truth in him. When he speaketh a lie, he speaketh
of his own: for he is a liar, and the father of it.

—*John 8:44 (KJV)*

In 2 Corinthians 2:11, the apostle Paul writes, "Lest Satan
should get an advantage of us: for we are not ignorant of
his devices" (KJV). In other words, for believers, the agenda,
tactics, and strategies of our enemy, Satan, are no longer a
mystery. There is no reason why the devil should get the best of
us. The amplified version of this passage says, "To keep Satan
from getting the advantage over us; for we are not ignorant of
his wiles and intentions."

Now that God through His Son Jesus Christ has made it

possible for us to be fully aware of the devil's devices, it is our responsibility to remain diligent in our efforts to understand our adversary's agenda. Ignorance of the devil's work can be fatal. Consider the words of Hosea 4:6:

> My people are destroyed for lack of knowledge: because thou hast rejected knowledge, I will also reject thee, that thou shalt be no priest to me: seeing thou hast forgotten the law of thy God, I will also forget thy children. (KJV)

It is my sincere belief that one of the challenges facing today's families is the lack of knowledge of the devil's schemes and tactics. Oftentimes, we approach our law situation with mere human perspective, and the Bible teaches us as believers that such a perspective is a contradiction to the way that God instructs us to view conflict and adversity. For the Bible says:

> For we wrestle not against flesh and blood, but against principalities, against powers, against the rulers of the darkness of this world, against spiritual wickedness in high places. (Ephesians 6:12 KJV)

In John 8:44, Jesus teaches His disciples concerning the nature of the devil. This passage of scripture reveals to us that not only is our adversary (the devil) a liar, but also "the father of a lie." In essence, he is the caretaker of the lies he attempts

to instill in the hearts and minds of believers until the lie has become our life-governing reality. This passage of scripture also reveals the patience and persistence of the devil. For example, let us consider the devil's approach in the garden of Eden:

> Now, the serpent was more subtil than any beast of the field, which the Lord God had made. And he said unto the woman, Yea, hath God said, ye shall not eat of every tree of the garden? And the woman said unto the serpent, We may not eat of the fruit of the trees of the garden: But of the fruit of the tree which is in the midst of the garden, God hath said, Ye shall not eat of it, neither shall ye touch it, lest ye die. And the serpent said unto the woman, Ye shall not surely die: For God doth know that in the day ye eat thereof, then your eyes shall be opened, and ye shall be as gods, knowing good and evil. (Genesis 3:1–5 KJV)

In this dialogue between Eve and the serpent (the vessel the devil used to lie to and deceive Eve), we see a willingness and a patience to ensure that Eve is fully persuaded and convinced of the lie that he is telling. The main attribute of the serpent that Genesis speaks of is his subtlety. By definition, the word *subtle* means "to be fine or delicate in meaning or intent; to be difficult to perceive or understand; requiring mental acuteness or discernment; cunning, wily, or crafty; to be skillful, clever, or ingenious." (dictionary.

com) In essence, the agenda that the serpent conveys is difficult for Eve to perceive because he is clever, cunning, and exceptionally skillful in his manner of deceiving her.

For example, consider the serpent's initiation of the dialogue with Eve. He cleverly initiates a dialogue that places her attention on the tree that God has put off limits. In addition to getting Eve's attention on the restricted tree, the serpent also manages to hold Eve's attention as he contradicts the word of God. These are the same strategies that the devil uses to attack and destroy our families. He distracts our attention from the will of God, and then he contradicts the word of God.

The impact of the serpent's agenda can be seen in the blame game many of our families play today. In Genesis 3:12–13, we read:

> And the man said, the woman whom thou gavest to be with me, she gave me of the tree, and I did eat. And the Lord God said unto the woman, what is this that thou hast done? And the woman said, The serpent beguiled me, and I did eat. (KJV)

In this passage of scripture, we see what happens when we allow Satan to get the advantage of our view of reality. In verse 12, we see Adam pointing to his beloved wife as the source of disobedience. It is amazing how fast our reality can be distorted once we allow the adversary to get our attention. Genesis 3:13 reveals that same attitude of blame in Eve that existed in Adam, as she shifts the blame to the serpent.

CHAPTER 4

Hope for the Home

And he shall go before him in the spirit and power of
Elias, turn the hearts of the fathers to the children,
and the disobedient to the wisdom of the just; to
make ready a people prepared for the Lord.
                                        —*Luke 1:17 (KJV)*

As we consider God's intentions, the devil's agenda, and
the current troublesome conditions of many of our
homes, we are led to ask the following questions: "Is there any
hope for our families?" and "If there is hope, what is the hope?"
The answer to the first question is simply and emphatically *yes*.
Yes, there is hope for our families against the devil's agenda to
destroy us. The source of our hope is the Lord, who never ceases
to reign. As believers, it is important that we understand the
order of God, in that He always goes second.

For example, in the beginning, the Bible introduces the

world in darkness first, then God speaks light into the dark world second. Consider that God allows Adam to eat of the forbidden tree first, then God makes atonement for Adam's sin second. Therefore, considering that God does not change— as we read in Malachi 3:6, "For I am the Lord, I change not; therefore ye sons of Jacob are not consumed" (KJV)—it is my sincere belief that in the order of God, He has in place a prevailing response to the devil's agenda and attack.

As we consider Luke 1:17, we see God's remedy to the attacks of our enemy. At first glance, we see the fulfillment of prophecy concerning John the Baptist (the forerunner to Jesus Christ) as his father Zacharias speaks to the angelic messenger of the Lord in Malachi 4:5–6:

> Behold, I will send you Elijah the prophet before the coming of the great and dreadful day of the Lord: And he shall turn the heart of the fathers to the children, and the heart of the children to their fathers, lest I come and smite the earth with a curse. (KJV)

It is my belief that beyond the dialogue between the angel and Zacharias, the passage in Luke 1:17 speaks of a movement of God that will restore our homes before the return of our Lord Jesus Christ. Consider that both Malachi 4:5–6 and Luke 1:17 speak of God's ministering to families as prior to His manifestation upon the earth. It is my belief in the movement

of God that serves as my hope for the troublesome times many of our families are facing.

The reality that many of us are dealing with as parents and children is that there seems to be resistance and conflict in our families that is greater than we can bear and beyond our comprehension. However, as believers, we have the word of God as our comfort, our war strategy, and our victory. For as the word of God declares in 2 Corinthians 1:3–4:

> Blessed be God, even the Father of our Lord Jesus Christ, the Father of mercies, and the GOD OF ALL COMFORT; Who comforteth us in all our tribulations, that we may able to comfort them which are in trouble, by the comfort wherewith we ourselves are comforted of God. (KJV)

The Bible also tells us in Ephesians 6:10–13 that our true source of strength and power is the Lord; also, that the true source of our conflicts and adversity is not humanity, as we perceive, but rather evil spiritual influences. Finally, the Bible declares in 1 John 4:4 that "Ye are of God, little children, and have OVERCOME them: because greater is he that is in you, than he that is in the world" (KJV). It is for these reasons that I believe that the same God who made His people ready for the first coming of our Lord Jesus Christ with John the Baptist— who came in the spirit and power of Elias—is preparing a remnant of vessels to carry that same anointing to minister to the needs of today's warring and hurting families.

As believers, it is critical that we not only keep the faith but also keep our hearts sensitive to God's desire to restore us as well as our families. I say this because oftentimes, as members of a broken home, we are wounded, and if we are not careful, our wounds can make us bitter and in turn harden our hearts. As a result of this pain and bitterness, we distance ourselves from our families in an attempt to protect ourselves. However, the word of the Lord declares it is God's desire to heal us of our pain and restore our brokenness. The only way we will ever allow God to heal us and restore our families is if we are convinced of His strength in our weakness, the success of His strategy, and the certainty of our victory in Jesus Christ.

CHAPTER 5

Kingdom Battles

There are very few individuals in the Bible with more pages dedicated to them than King David, second king of Israel. From his youth to his final days as king, there is so much written about him. The Bible records that David was a shepherd boy who fought against some of the wilderness' great predators. It also reports that David was a great musician who faithfully served King Saul during times of spiritual warfare and distress and that he courageously and successfully defended the nation of Israel and the name of the true and living God against the giant Goliath. King David is a wonderful example of a gifted and courageous vessel who strived to honor God with his gifts and his life.

However, as with many of us, there are chapters in David's life that show the vulnerability of his humanity and his need for grace from God, patience with himself, and mercy toward others. Following David's affair with Bathsheba and his role in

the death of her husband, Uriah, God sent a messenger to get his attention. One of the components of God's message to David is the reality of conflict within his family. As 2 Samuel 12:10 states, "Now, therefore, the sword shall never depart from your house, because you despised me and took the wife of Uriah the Hittite to be your own" (KJV).

One of the most captivating aspects of the judgment against the home of King David is the life of his son Absalom. The Bible introduces us to Absalom following the rape of King David's daughter, Tamar. Absalom decides to avenge his sister by killing the rapist—his brother Ammon.

For a moment, imagine being King David, facing the daunting task of leading God's people when you receive notice that your daughter has been sexually assaulted and the perpetrator is one of your sons. As you and your family are working to recover from the traumatic experience of your children being involved in such a terrible event, you receive notification that one of your sons has been murdered by another son.

Following the traumatic death of Ammon at the hands of Absalom, King David decides to banish Absalom from the kingdom of Israel. Regardless of the political responsibilities that David has as king, there exists an undeniable reality that as a husband and a father, he is trying to manage the vast number of needs of his family as well as his nation following the decisions made by his sons Ammon and Absalom.

Later, on the advice of his nephew Joab, David decides to invite Absalom back to the kingdom of Israel. It is important

that while the Bible records the return of Absalom, it does not record his reconciliation with his father. This is important to note because the Bible does record that following his return to the kingdom of Israel, Absalom works to gain the favor of the people of Israel with the hope of taking the throne from his father. It is recorded that the takeover plot of Absalom grew to the degree that King David was forced to retreat from the threat placed on his life. The takeover plot concludes with the death of Absalom, who was killed by his cousin Joab (the one who advocated for his return to the kingdom).

The household of King David serves an example of so many lessons, including the following:

- Royalty cannot shield you from trauma and conflict.
- Even gifted and important people deal with great problems.
- You can be successful publicly and struggle privately at home.
- Children who have access to good training and countless resources will still make bad decisions.
- When trauma happens to one member of a family, it happens to every member of a family.
- At some point, you will offend your family member(s). Be prepared to reconcile with one another.

- There are times when, behind closed doors, people are considering painful plots against members of their family.
- People who God uses can make bad choices privately that can and will affect them publicly.
- The call of God on an individual's life includes moments of hardship, trauma, and conflict.
- The enemy of our faith intends to make us believe that we are "sleeping with the enemy."

My prayer for every family is that we never lose sight of the imperfections that we harbor as we live and encounter each other.

My prayer is that we will discover the grace to forgive when our pain tells us to harbor hard feelings toward our offenders, especially those we are related to.

My prayer is that parents not only find the will to provide for their children but work to be and remain reconciled with their children.

My prayer is that children always hold their parents in honor and respect.

My prayer is that families take the energy of hostility toward each other and direct it to the enemy of faith in activities of fasting and prayer.

My prayer is that families always see their call to one another and never see each other as enemies.

Printed in the United States
By Bookmasters